"One writes out of one thing only—one's own experience. Everything depends on how relentlessly one forces from this experience the last drop, sweet or bitter, it can possibly give. This is the only real concern of the artist, to recreate out of the disorder of life that order which is art."

— James Baldwin, *Notes of a Native Son*

at the core of these notes is sage commentary on leading a meaningful and healthy existence with yourself and others. life, love, and happiness are vital for the soul which serves as our bodies' rich soil: as planters need fertile soil to grow crops, our souls need special ingredients to thrive.

NOTES OF A DENVER NATIVE SON

OTHER WORKS BY ADRIAN MICHAEL

loamexpressions

Blinking Cursor

The Art of Self-Publishing

NOTES OF A DENVER NATIVE SON

ADRIAN MICHAEL

POETRY + PROSE
ON LIFE, LOVE, AND HAPPINESS

Published by A.Michael Ventures | Denver, CO
Chapter illustration by Eljay Higley
Book layout and design by GreenHigley

To contact the author visit adrianmichaelgreen.com

ISBN-13: 978-1499665536
ISBN-10: 1499665539

Printed in the United States of America

snow-capped rockies
mountains to the west
expect four seasons
all in one day.
interstate seventy
cuts across the country
connecting travelers
from utah to maryland.
denver our capital
standing a mile high
front range our backyard
a sight for sore eyes.
rio colorado
the river for which we are named
a spanish explorers claim
for the red colored silt the river lays.
the centennial state
installed in 1876
ulysses s. grant our president
made us 38th.
asset and civil union
recently just passed
granting equal liberty
we should be proud.
a rich history exists
spanning hundreds of years
denver native
honored to say.
denver my heart
forever more.

to my city

loam (lom) n.

1. a rich soil or mixture, especially one composed of clay, silt and sand
2. proportioned ingredients for one's soul to thrive in a given existence

notes of a denver native son is a book of poetic affirmations on life, love and happiness. growing up in colorado, i have always been surrounded by storytellers and historians who made it a point to pass on lessons that were passed on to them. a storyteller myself, i hope to share out what i have learned, and what i continue to learn, to those who are willing to listen.

my notes are based off of three main topics that i have found myself writing about the past two years. in those two years my partner has gifted me with beautiful insight just by simply being her own natural self and it is fitting that this book falls on the bend of when we first spent time together.

the poetry and prose herein are saturated with my experiences, with honesty, and my concern as an artist to recreate the disorder of my life, my observations, to an order which is art. "native son" is poetic by nature because i was raised by poetry.

in the infancy of this book i had another title in mind. as it evolved i couldn't help but think of the late great James Baldwin and his 1955 classic, "notes of a native son" which i had read my senior year in high school; i wanted to pay tribute to his influence in literature and life.

these notes remind me to appreciate the air in my lungs, the stable ground beneath my feet, and opportunities to hear, taste, touch, see, feel and explore the world and my relationship with myself and others.

life, love and happiness are my clay, silt, and sand. if i have nothing, then in my words i have everything; may you find your loam and lead a purposed and meaningful existence. perhaps mine might serve as a basic foundation.

i hope you take in the following poetry and prose to further cultivate and nourish the soul that so desperately wants to come up for air.

Adrian Michael
July 4, 2014

NOTES OF A DENVER NATIVE SON

NOTES OF A DENVER NATIVE SON

pretty things
jammed way 'neath the earth
yearn quietly
to be discovered

dirt
atop buried gems
serves as a protective shield
making it difficult to be revealed

dormant it sleeps
cast in the dark
hidden
desperate to be found out

wake up
wake up
something inside you yells
are you ready to listen?

your soul is crying out

on life

mirrors
i look
not
for reflection
of myself
but to see
angles and sides
of what
surrounds me
to
observe beauty
easily
taken for
granted

Adrian Michael

presence
coefficient

there have only been a few times that i can recall being 100% present to the moment. the last time was when i was sitting in the cold arkansas river; and the first was free-falling out of an airplane in the sky. in those distinctive moments there was clarity and no distraction. the now was more important than worrying about other things that i could be doing. perhaps it was the nature element that cleared my mind that connected, so vividly connected, me to the surroundings free of anything else. find ways to facilitate being present and orient yourself such that it drowns out distractions. to be in the moment radiates calm enjoyment that, with practice, becomes second nature and eradicates stressors; in return you will find each moment to be fulfilling like fresh water and cool air.

Adrian Michael

the detail
dividend

pay attention, close minute attention, to those you love. ask questions, be curious, and listen to their stories. the details you will learn and uncover will reveal the unspoken gaps in your relationship and strengthen its connection. be genuine; explore beyond the surface and the detail dividend, life's pay off, will light up your existence bringing us all closer together.

Adrian Michael

fresh paint

you can put up new walls
paint and renovate.
import the best glass,
expensive,
to please the finest taste.
new chairs,
curtains,
upholstery
the works
everything brand new—
built to revamp
a new you.
an outward approach
does nothing for
what needs to happen within.
so take inventory
honest and true
what is it that you see?
i doubt buying new things
will do anything.
look inside
good
bad
flaws and all.
work inside out
compass yourself about.
the end result,
though the journey may be long,
will be worthwhile;
fresh paint only covers and hides,
a quick fix deluxe
do yourself a favor, pop the hood
roll up your sleeves
get to work

Adrian Michael

leadershift

if i pass you the ball will you know what to do with it? out with the age old 'look to the leader' for all answers and perspectives, and in with multi-dimensional insights. we each have a role to play and must step up to the challenge when it's our turn to carry the load, especially when others are counting on us. no longer can we sit idle waiting for another to do the work and anticipate full benefits; instead let's lend a hand, offer up a talent or skill and contribute. as we venture to better ourselves and our surroundings it will take a leadershift from one person to the next, maximizing everyone to get to the next level.

Adrian Michael

courage

it takes courage, a considerable amount of mental strength, to endure life's battles. there is so much capacity within that nothing should hold you back; not fear, danger or difficulty. the gold that is you must go through the fire, not to burn, but for the purpose of removing obstacles that keep you from shining. it takes courage under fire to venture, endure and persevere—
and to do it all over again.

Adrian Michael

passion

what do you enjoy most and are you engaging or running away from it? our daily lives are often filled with monotony and even with hours to spare upon release from the job we are too tired, too drained, too exhausted to do anything; and then we wake up and suffer the monotony again. i've heard that we "all" can't do what we love and that we "all" have responsibilities that take priority over what we really want to be doing. there is no time to postmark your passion for today in hopes for it to manifest tomorrow.

pursuing anything takes a plan of action, just saying you 'want' or 'will' can only get you so far. embed what you love doing in the hours that you have, not the hours you haven't accrued. i am a firm believer that you make time for things you care about whether it be people, hobbies or sport. do yourself a favor and pursue passion as if your life depended on it, because it does! with no passion there is the mundane and you deserve so much better.

Adrian Michael

pressure

pressure may bring discomfort, an overwhelming burden of physical or mental distress. the pressure to be perfect; the pressure to be successful; the pressure to be the best; the pressure to win; the pressure to conform... are all but few of many manmade dispositions. why is it that so much weight is placed on what others think? is it the validation that comes with it to be accepted and being part of the fold? or do we even know anymore?

real pressure is a test felt by the individual who measures past battles with present circumstance and the ability to see self improvement. the pressures of what is popular is but a game of shadows and up to us to value our own paths without compare.

Adrian Michael

loyalty

loyalty goes a long way. it is an unswerving allegiance, a faithful due diligence, to your ambition and aspirations. a promise that must be kept. loyalty will be the necessary fuel to get closer to your goals. quitting is easy but regret lasts forever: don't give up when things get hard, remember the commitment you made to yourself and see it through.

Adrian Michael

resolutions

resolve: a goal without a plan is the sabotage of any resolution.
at the turn of each year we reflect on what we did and didn't,
wished and wanted. there is always that one thing, always one,
that never seems to get accomplished. be it a habit, routine,
outlook or dream, it is never realized. sure, the first couple
of days and weeks your mind is set on your resolution(s) but
without understanding that it's a process, an intentional act
of analyzing each goal and its purpose, it will go unresolved.
to be resolute in intention you must be reasonable, clear, and
determined as you name your problems/ambitions followed by
steadfast solution. you are the answer to all that you want to see
and be, get out the way of your self.

Adrian Michael

rabble

rouser

such fortitude and selfless ambition define those who wish to leave a legacy—but not just any legacy. a people's history will always be flanked with a spectrum of individuals who carelessly put their self interest on the line for the greater cause for others to reap benefits of a better and full life. there is a brilliant audacity to leave a legacy where those that come after you can only speak in compliment and praise no matter how hard attempts may be to discount and ridicule. to the pioneers across all walks of life who made those first steps onto unpaved territories; to the rabble rousers who questioned the status quo; to the visionaries who believed in a better tomorrow; to the people from humble beginnings who strived to be successful to help their family; to the risk takers who said we could do this ourselves; to each humanitarian champion known and unknown, thank you for not giving up—your legacy will not be forgotten so long as we keep your names on our lips, you will never cease to exist. i just hope the legacy i leave makes you proud.

Adrian Michael

regret

i don't know why but there is a force or pressure to hold back
just enough to keep people (and ourselves) at bay. perhaps there
are deep painful wounds lodged on our psyche that causes us to
distrust kindness; maybe the trauma cuts so indescribably that it
shattered any hope for a better situation to come after. regardless
of what happened let the past be past. you might be able to count
the days that have come and gone but tomorrow, tomorrow is a
check you might not be able to cash. so that phone call you have
been meaning to give, dial the number now; that trip you've been
wanting to take, plan it now; that hug you've been holding back,
wrap your arms around someone real tight; and those words
you've been scared to say, let 'em rip! the games we play with
ourselves will be the barriers to our own happiness.
satisfy the thirst to live with no regrets.

Adrian Michael

difference

i want to be exceptionally different and not like anyone else. not that i think i am better than anyone but when you recognize that you are uniquely built there is an intrinsic desire to set out on your own path. in business to be successful they say you must have a competitive advantage; in sports they say to win you must be better than your opponent. it is natural to study the moves and techniques of others but trend setters think multiple moves ahead and operate in spaces where little thought has been given. i will push the envelope to the best of my ability so that by the time i get where i am supposed to be, success and competitive advantage will be measured by how exceptionally different each of us can be.

Adrian Michael

convenience

at the corner sits most convenience stores,
operating 24 hours a day. they offer your basic
necessities: fuel, food, and other things. there are
people who see you as a convenience store—
they never show their faces until they desperately
need you or whenever they so choose to make
time and just pop up. it is easy to treat someone
like they mean nothing and use them to fill a
temporary void and it is easy to think nothing of
it. you never want to be someone's convenience
store, they drain you mentally and physically—
all they will do is strip you bare and only return
when you re-stock rather than stick around and
replenish the shelves alongside you. it's up to you
to learn when to refuse service to someone and
recognize convenience shoppers
when they walk through the door.

Adrian Michael

darkness
dwellers

darkness does nothing but make your eyes adjust to the
absence of direct light. no matter the circumstance of low
or high visibility, there is an intense influence, an allure of
sorts, that nests a comfort of the unknown. it takes practice
to navigate in the dark to avoid pitfalls, the challenge in that
is some have mastered navigating pitfalls they have become
a sweet spot—an ill intentioned dwelling known for hurting
others. you can try and shed light on someone's actions all
you want, but it is on them
to the see the darkness in their ways.

Adrian Michael

spirituality

don't be afraid to grow! as
i am blessed to rise another day
it's as if i learn a small piece
about myself that peaks through.
look into the inner you, surround
yourself with positive people and
positive energy; connect with the powers
that you believe in. knowing that the
universe conspires with your every intention
is motivation enough to plug into
your soul and honor it; spirituality
is a personal journey.

Adrian Michael

be yourself

trying to be someone else is a learned behavior. everywhere you turn it looks like this place is being overrun by clones. let's get back to doing things because we want to or because we like it, not because we saw it on tv or because there is pressure to conform. be original or find that the custom made soul within your physical body will die the further away you leave the authentic self towards trying to replicate who you were never meant to be. if we were meant to look, sound, think and feel the same, we would, but we aren't and that's what makes living so beautiful. honor yourself by being yourself.

i
think deeply
to purge
and venture
within
not really
sure
if i've
found
what
exactly
i'm looking
for

this place
i've only known
so
i
must cherish
what i have
breathe
slowly
and
exhale

a solemn
story
i do not
have
but
we all
bleed;
we all
bleed

Adrian Michael

memory loss
scares me;
i hope
memories
will last
once my
pen
reaches
the
pad

looking
for
myself
amongst
the sway
of chaos
takes
time;
what
shall be
will
be
sometimes
we must
be selfish

my ebon skin
has seen grand things
its history on
heiroglyph walls and
obelisk landscapes
near great pyramids
and the river nile
this skin
is rich
with sun that
beams from
within

skin of wonder
these pours pour
struggle and triumph
stretch marked on
my back
to
never
forget

life
for me
aint been
no crystal stair
yet
the landings
i've stood on
have less
tacks and splinters
some carpet
has been laid
but i can't
stop now
too many
have died
sacrificed lives
to get to the top
a place
we all
have yet to see

i couldn't sleep last night.
anxiety rested in my stomach
and
my mind replayed a verdict that
sent chills of disbelief.
what would huey do?
what would malcolm say?
angela, ella, rosa...
what can we do?
trayvon martin will be sixteen years and twenty-one days, forever.
shot and killed bearing arms with
skittles and a can of fruit punch
there is reasonable doubt in my soul of the justice system
a system built on oppression, exploitation and violence.
let us
  stand
let us
  unite
let us
  pray;
prayer can move mountains.
i closed my eyes with sadness in my heart
i open them with appreciation for life
coupled in fear—
black man,
do not be afraid.
stand in your power
protect your domain
continue to walk in the rain

for trayvon

be still
my grandmother
used to say

i always
had somewhere
to go
but never
knew where

i own those words
and seek to be still

when
bark
from this tree
grows
brittle and torn
i pray
the roots
far extend
to another

i wrote for others
to rant and rave
hoping validation
would come
so i could come back
and brag to my words
on how good they were
and pat myself
on the back

i no longer write for others
i write for you
so what keeps your mind racing
leaves temporarily
and stains and poisons
another medium
tasting brisk oxygen
to form new combinations
with other words expunged

i write for you
my soul
in hopes
that you
write back

can i share
to you
my deepest
secrets
and walk
out of the
darkness
hand in hand
with them
and...
there is no and
but a request:
judge not
and hold
all
of my dark
pieces
as you would
hold
my light

Adrian Michael

election day
spent with my
older brother

watched
silly videos
on his
hospital bed

those
weeks
scary
him fighting
pnemonia

no matter
the outcome
of our
two-term
president
i was
happy
and bonded
to the
life
of my brother

two victories
his health
and an
election

clenched
fists
and prayers
newfound
appreciation
for life
for life

we drew on walls
my twin brother and i
he was always more creative

running around
the front and back yard
our domain to tame

nothing was off limits
not even the window
to the garage
that somehow got broke

big wheels &
skateboards
our mobiles of choice

happiness lived in those moments
on garfield and 28th

mr. horton
our old neighbor
lived across the street
decked in blue jump suits
his wrinkles and smile
i remember his accent
alike sir ray charles

ms. lee to our left
sat always in her yard
observing the neighborhood
and waving was her sport

Adrian Michael

o, how we played
until the street lights came on
little sister was always with us
pigtails and barrettes
her curly hair glistened in the sun

the one-story duplex
was our red-brick castle
had its share of war and peace treaties
it weathered the storm

what we had
small and modest
was special and humble
all i could ever wish for

a place called home
in denver colorado

on love

a love
like
elizabeth & castro
is what
i've always
wanted

they would
sit and talk
for hours
in the
kitchen
on those
rickety gray
wood-panel
chairs

he parked his car
in the alley
outside the gate
and brought in
countless bags
of groceries
the grandkids
were sure to eat

they never
fought or complained
though i'm sure
that isn't true
but from them
i learned
love &
affection

life stripped us
of elizabeth
our grandmother dear
and castro (our abuelito)
took with him
her ashes
and spread them
in their fave ocean
to a country near

always together
eventhough she's
gone
i carry with me
the love they shared

i see it in
the ripples and bubbles
waves and blues

for betty

Adrian Michael

life line

your partner is a life line—they support you in all things and give of themselves. trust the process of their love as it unfolds. it latches on to you like a harness and won't let go: soon you will teeter on tight ropes, leap from plank to plank, swing on wobbly bridges and though sometimes you may feel uncertain, nervous, scared, or vulnerable, your partner encourages you, your partner will do anything to lift you as you climb. don't take advantage of a life line, you can't assume that you will have another to choose from.

be a life line that is unquestionable.

Adrian Michael

deep end

love is not shallow, for its ocean is far too vast and far too deep. there are many ways to learn how to swim and in those methods come technique, skill, and discipline to maneuver in the water. failure to adhere to certain guidelines could be a fatal risk so proper precaution and due diligence must be adhered to.

love is like water: powerful enough to drown you and soft enough to cleanse you. to master love you must respect and study its majesty like you would learning to swim and prove you are ready to swim in the deep end.

skyland was where i learned to swim. every summer we were signed up to take swimming lessons at the local recreation center in park hill. our grandmother would walk the three of us from her home on ivy street early in the morning. we carried our bathing suits wrapped in towels.

our instructors taught us how to hold our breath under water, how to tread water, how to float, the front crawl, backstroke, breaststroke, sidestroke, and eventually how to carry those skills in the deep end. every kid wanted to swim in the deep end, but not everyone was equipped with the basic skills to be in that part of the pool.

to prove readiness we were tested by our ability to swim the width of the pool and tread (keeping our head above water) for an extended amount of time. passing that test gave us full access and rights to the diving board and slide to plunge ourselves in 9-feet-deep glorious blue water.

the beauty in those lessons are carried with me today. it isn't just about being able to swim, it is beyond that. the objectives give life skills transferrable to anything and everything especially to that of love:

love is an ocean that tests your ability to swim, breathe, dive, slide, tread, float, and maneuver. at any time clear skies can become grey and a storm will wage mighty winds to prove yourself, your commitment, your faith, your loyalty, your trust, your discipline, your love, your everything.

it is of no surprise that some still cannot swim. there is a fear of water, fear of potentially drowning, fear of the unknown. no one took the time to show them how or they only had the opportunity to observe from afar. love should be tested before we enter the waves of life and relationships. perhaps we would have less shipwrecks and broken hearts.

love should be taught and never played with.

it is never too late to learn how to swim.

Adrian Michael

decades
kind

i recognize that every relationship is different and unique. i do not want what is gossiped about in magazines or retweeted on a minifeed. i do not want the cookie cutter romance hyped up by the masses who don't understand the hard hitting sludge matches that occur for everything to appear perfect. rather than glorify celebrity screenshots and out-of-context famous quotes, i will think about my people who might never read this message because they are too busy strengthening their marriages. i want that decades kind of love when each finger counted means 10 years; to smile and laugh when looking back fifty years; to kiss my life partner to celebrate all the countless moments; to get through fights and add photos to the wall; to turn over each day shedding tears of joy, thankful for being able to share this love and life with someone else. declare what love you want and need, and watch it find its way to you. but what you ask for, you must work for; love doesn't work for you.

Adrian Michael

romance

romance is a two-way street. it is the
practice of conscious acts of kindness
used to remind the one you love how
significant their presence is.

the moment you stop saying thank
you to one another is the moment
the candles of your flamed romance
begin to flicker. be spontaneous, be
thoughtful, be in love—keep your
appreciation of the mind, body and
soul at the forefront of
your love affair.

Adrian Michael

rid yourself

when you find someone who makes you want to be better, hold onto them. not because you would be a fool to let them go, but because they serve a greater purpose that doesn't make sense until later on. these people aren't like the math or science classes you hated in school but come to find out to be of some use down the road—they are the teachers who exert so much energy supporting your dreams; the nurses that bring you back to full health when you are sick; the cheerleaders saying 'you can do it' in your ear; the best friends that keep it real; those that are still standing when the dust clears. yes, we all have to be accountable for ourselves, our actions, our everything, but in this lifetime there is a calming effect on our being when those we surround ourselves with have genuine spirits and easy-going aura, something to emulate. rid yourself of people who pull you down rather than lift you up, or else bare witness to a soul wasted.

Adrian Michael

be open

10 + 1

1) shortness of breath
2) unable to put into words what you want to say
3) putting your partners needs before your own
4) can't help but smile whenever they are around
5) leave early when out with your boys/girls to go home just to sit next to him/her
6) call them countless times throughout the day just to hear their voice
7) start to anticipate them when they get off work
8) enjoy the small things they do that used to bother you
9) check your phone seconds after you put it down to see if they messaged you back
10) write poem after poem professing your adoration
11) realizing you found the best friend that has been looking for you, too

these are some symptoms of love that might come about—they may sound juvenile, simple or just plain lame. trust me, i was a skeptic as well, but the more you open yourself up to the possibilities you deserve, you'll see a shift in how you see this thing called love.

Adrian Michael

fantasy

in our hearts they poured
images
songs
tales
of fantasy
of far-fetched happenings
spoon-fed like medicine
i became disillusioned
picture perfect love is a feaux
and it took years to shed
love is as real as
the dust collection on vhs cassettes
it's what you make it
go off your own script
live it
don't memorize it;
my fantasy
is
knowing
hard days gon' come
making loves bond
strong

Adrian Michael

spontaneity

the mundane is easy to fall into:
long days at work and all you feel
like doing is keeping company with
netflix and watching the hours go by
- we all do it - catch up on shows
and binge. how many hours do you
spend checking facebook, twitter,
instagram? challenge yourself to
put technology down and work on a
project that you have been meaning
to complete. surprise yourself and
be spontaneous with the use of
time; say yes to productivity and no
to idleness.

24 hours in a day, 168 hours in a
week, don't wait to live. your partner
will thank you for it; your soul
will be satisfied.

Adrian Michael

compromise

your partner does not always do
what you want to do because
they like it, they do it because
of the joy it brings being next
to you, spending quality time.
push and pull, give and take.
relationships typically struggle
because one person wants to
be in control, but control is
just temporary greed that will
leave you alone and bankrupt:
make decisions together, a rela-
tionship is a shared experience.

Adrian Michael

perseverence

whenever people are involved it's going to get hard. blood boiling, eyes rolling, balled fists, fed up type of emotions will make you lose your cool. do you fight or do you flee? in my experience it is easier to head to the hills, call it quits and avoid putting in work. however, to persevere, to stand and face the storm, muster enough courage and respect not just to do patchwork but to strengthen the foundation and trust each other to not run when the next storm comes.

Adrian Michael

beyond

repair

how do you navigate a situation that is best for both of you to part ways? trouble is, too often people stay in toxic relationships knowing they deserve better, but would rather settle than leave out to the unknown. no matter how many conversations and broken promises there is a point when it is beyond repair. in fact, there probably was one (or more) red flag in the beginning that went unaddressed that now has become a major issue. if a car is leaking oil, take it in to the shop; you mitigate future problems by addressing/taking care of it before it can get worse. reflect on what you need and want, hurry before it's too late.

Adrian Michael

loving
yourself

be unconditional and own every flaw, perk, strength and weakness that is you. think about it, you are with you all day every day and rather than investing all of that time looking for love from others, divert that energy into yourself. you know the love that you deserve — you are the only constant in this equation because when others leave, all you have is yourself. if you rely on the love of someone else to lead a meaningful life, then you will forever be at their mercy. love on some you.

Adrian Michael

loving
others

once you have mastered the art of loving yourself, then it radiates outward. the process of loving yourself will be recognized, perhaps even misunderstood, by people you interact with on a daily basis. loving yourself will spark attention from people you may have never met before, but they are drawn to you. by loving yourself, loving others naturally seeps out of your pours and it is meant to be shared. to love is a selfless act that you must conquer individually and the ripple effect will naturally impact others, even if they don't want to accept it.

Adrian Michael

loving

&

leading

to love is to cherish, to lead is to give direction. you should never lead astray someone you love or provide false hope. the games people play at first might seem fun and harmless but recognize the damage that is being done. be true to yourself and live in truth or see the make-shift walls of your relationship come crashing down.

it becomes intentional foolishness when you know your words are full of lies, think twice before entering other lives. let go or hold onto, a choice simply yours, but only lead the one you love in honest direction; know the difference or prepare being a heartbreaker or the heartbroken.

Adrian Michael

perfection

everyone looking for the perfect relationship but don't want to put in the work. at the first sign of chaos the ship is abandoned before it's necessary to jump overboard. the perfect relationship, the one that to the outside world looks polished, pretty, and pristine, is a facade. being without fault or defect is an ambitious aspiration that quite honestly is something i don't want. i want to argue over silly things and get mad from time to time and struggle in the trenches to make our bond stronger.

a perfect relationship is the culmination of love and friendship that stands together each and every time a strong headwind tries to capsize the ship you are steering and both of you never let go until the waters become clear again. you may never see the storm in someone's relationship but know that the perfect ship has to fight like hell to stay afloat.

Adrian Michael

communication

let's be clear: we say that we value communication when things need to be discussed rather than left unspoken. but, be honest. communication in a barebones state, is all about vulnerability, stating information, feelings, judgements, and wants that may not be fully heard or appreciated.

try something on for a moment. *what is the risk you take by avoiding expressing yourself to a partner, friend, colleague, or stranger? what is the risk you take by opening up to them? what is the risk you take by shutting down their desire to communicate?* the process of communication is about being heard and understood. by keeping things to yourself they end up becoming toxic and build up to eventually explode. you've seen it happen.

many relationships end because one or both of you were unwilling to express yourselves or your feelings. an argument is healthy dialogue to convey thoughts and/or actions that need clarification. a fight, on the other hand, is when you are unwilling to listen. one can lead you into unproductive space and the other can lead you into productive space.

let. go. let go of those words you have been meaning to say. if you value your own mental and physical well-being you will see and utilize communication as a tool to release heavy burdens that fog your soul, that tense your mood, that haunt your psyche.

feedback is good. no one is perfect. once you own and agree to open communication be prepared to hear some things that may sting, cut, or blindside. keep in mind we all interpret the world through many different lenses and if communication is clear and direct, words will be heard, relationships will be strengthened and love will prevail.

that is the point, afterall. love yourself enough to verbalize an experience that may not have felt right, share out what someone said or did that you would like to honor and celebrate, state what you want and the universe will see it through.

be willing to listen attentively.
be willing to talk genuinely.
give and receive.

Adrian Michael

i don't know how you did it
but you did
raising three kids

we were a handful

you made ends meet
providing for us
you bought your first home
we had our own rooms

so beautiful you are
a soul so gentle and kind

i can't thank you enough

they say i'm goofy
i get it from you
they say i dress well
i get it from you
they say i'm a gentleman
you taught me how
they say i'm sensitive
you taught me how
they say i'm giving
you taught me how

what i cherish most
is having a loving mother
who would do anything
for her kids

i aspire to pour into others
what you poured selflessly into me

NOTES OF A DENVER NATIVE SON

i have written about you
in a dark tulsan room
late nights
no sleep
writing for someone like you

no one understood
not even my self
but i kept writing and writing
journaled notes
i just couldn't see your face

years had past
the entries still remained
the moment i met you
i knew

i was writing about you

love
is knowing
yourself
inside and
out

love
is recognizing
each breath
you take
and filling
lungs to
capacity
and breathing
in again
til nothing
more
can seep in;

love
is holding
all that
air
and
letting
it all go

your eyes
how they
say
so much

beautiful flowers
lay across
those pupils

do you see them?

each blink
waters
those pretty floral petals

i have found
beauty
in many things
but
in this
a yawn
i've discovered
buried treasure;
the parting
of lips
drop of the chin
and mouth
wide open
is a gesture
from the
soul
breathing
love out

what if
love
was a
circle
that
withered
into a
heart?

***

the sun
has a way
of doing
what the
moon
commands

if you mind the gap between
my head and my heart
then you must stomach my sink
holes. if you withstand the ebbs and
flows of my moods then, and only
then, my dear
our moons eclipse

love
is
a
language
under
stood
without
words

Adrian Michael

she isn't broken
and her bones aren't delicate
the only fracture
is the break between her lips
and if she wills it
the space between air and sound
will let you in
and all she may need
is for you
to listen;
she has saved herself
far too many times
not everyone needs rescuing

love. it makes you want to clench
your fists, scream, get angry and
feel afraid. love. will push you in
the mud, get you dirty, and make
you work it all out. love. is not all
picture perfect and smiles. love is
rolling up your sleeves.

love is worth fighting for.

love
is magic
the kind that
hypnotizes the soul
& pinpoints
broken bones
& detached sinew;
love
is
the benevolent spell
that scoops
          up the pieces
making us whole
again

i'm an old soul
that believes in
chivalry, romance,
and love

Adrian Michael

leave space in your heart
when you think there's nothing left
let it be a reserve
for those that need it most

pay it forward with no expectation
of anything in return
humanity needs a new banking system
start depositing love

how you've
matured my soul
unscathed this tongue
uncovered dormant words;
loving you
is
loving myself
eternally grateful
our stars collided

***

when
she
lets
you
in
protect
her
heart

on happiness

so contagious
a smile
it sends
spinal sensations
felicity and content
converting
frowns to smirks

Adrian Michael

decisions

if your life flashed before your eyes
from the very beginning to where you are now
would you be proud of what you have done?
have you lived the way you set out?
what will you do to move forward?
ask yourself these questions and more
be accepting of decisions you've made
you are who you are because of them
yet, know it is in your supervision
to change direction
or stay the course

***

you are
who you are
and to me
no matter
how hard
you try
pretending
to be whole
i know you are
a broken puzzle
trying to find
all of the right pieces;
i honor
that part of you
yearning
to be put
back together

Adrian Michael

locus of
control

for many years i lost sleep because of
the power i let others have on me. words
cut deep, comments against my character
had me question everything, nothing i did
was ever good enough measured against
someone else's standards. during those
trying times i didn't have the courage to
speak up for myself, i stuttered over what
was racing in my head that i couldn't
concisely articulate, my mental health was
under attack and i had high anxiety. as life
happened, it tends to do it well, i stepped
into my confidence and developed a
stronger voice.

i may not have control of your actions,
i don't want to, but i know one thing is
for certain: why bother losing sleep over
something someone said or did when
they themselves are absolutely not losing
sleep over you? tossing and turning will
happen but never give your power away
to a person, place, or thing. if anything
be mindful of who you are and shrug off
what is out of your
locus of control.

Adrian Michael

invest

success is mostly defined on monetary gain and material
things. modesty is a life i aspire to maintain and flip
an outdated definition to fit contemporary well-being.
happiness, a true indicator of personal success, will outlive
the printed dollar. place value in your self and spend
time that is rightfully yours; invest in the economics of
happiness and watch, just watch, the difference it will
make in all of our lives.

Adrian Michael

silence

there is something about silence that used to make me uneasy and at times it still does. why is that? the absence of sound or any noise for that matter forces you to focus on something that is very easy to avoid—yourself. in silence you are confronted with what may be the things that need the most attention. keeping busy so that there is no time to reflect or unpack what is in your mind will only lead to bigger issues.

be still, meditate, and pinpoint that which consumes your energy and welcome silence as a helpful tool to find inner peace.

Adrian Michael

originality

each of us is an artist equipped with our own palette and brushes with a primed canvas. what was once a valuable trait to define ourselves has now become a rarity. there is a lot of cookie cutting going on, pre-made tools used to categorize us, shape us, control us. get back to the beauty of originality and don't be imitative of what you see; be independent and creative in thought and action. you are too unique to be placed in a box! so pick up your brush and re-create yourself, you are a work of art.

Adrian Michael

attitude

our thoughts frame how we see and navigate the world. it is a basic fact that any mental position with regard to what is going on around us will dictate how we interact. being around people with bad attitudes can be draining to the point you stop wanting to be around them and not attend any activity you know they will be at. their attitude has now granted control over what you do and how you live: you have now become an avoider. the positive thoughts and emotions have now been infiltrated by someone else's attitude when it shouldn't be a factor. it is human nature to not like to be around certain people but you shouldn't have to adjust the things you do to accommodate their attitude. never apologize for cutting out negative components of your life because the impact of attitude is a reflection of you.

***

there is nothing
selfish
about being
selective
with the company
you keep

Adrian Michael

stress

how restless do you find yourself
to be? at the core of it all anxiety is
at play, sort of an uneasy, on-edge
feeling. restlessness is a symptom of
anxiety. when you are restless there
is a surge of energy (adrenaline)
that moves throughout your body
but nothing is happening to get rid
of it. all that built up energy has to
be utilized in order to get back to
equilibrium, a calm state.
if you find yourself to be restless,
do something—move to accomplish
some thing. use all of that natural
energy to your advantage
with intent and purpose.

Adrian Michael

forgiveness

are you holding on so tight to something from your past that it manifests in your present? whatever it is that happened, let it go. no it won't be easy, and no it won't be easily forgotten, but your days are far more important than worrying about yesterday. forgive yourself and others for past actions, not because you were wrong and they were right, or vice versa, but because it will free up space for you to focus on something else. a burden will be lifted and you will start feeling different, no more anxiety or stress, relationships with be healthier and psychologically you will think straight. forgiveness is power that you control, a process to commit to; force the grip of the past to unhand you and witness a positive change in all dimensions of wellness.

Adrian Michael

the
scarlet
letter

"i" has become the new scarlet letter; not the stitched letter "a" worn for punishment and put on display for the public to see and judge. the letter "i" self defines and you must wear it with pride. step out with confidence and dignity despite the careless looks and stares; it is your life to live. the letter though invisible, is a badge of honor too many are afraid to wear. we gossip about what others wear, what they said, things they dared, and shake our heads. it's the risk you take but let the haters hate. get busy living and be yourself!

Adrian Michael

correlation

happiness is an experience you have to commit to by directly participating in it. don't live on the sidelines of your life waiting for something to happen. take one step towards happiness and happiness takes two steps towards you. a direct correlation exists between the way you live and the things that happen around you. it is on you to decide what that relationship looks like.

Adrian Michael

lessons

tendencies to overthink heighten anxiety
and in those moments we can miss seeing
clearly. worrying is natural but don't let it
devour the lesson: no matter how big
or small, find joy
in everything that comes your way.

Adrian Michael

listen

do what you enjoy most. perhaps pursuing a passion on a full-time basis may not be the smartest thing to do (right now), but if everyday you set aside time to do something you love, then you are managing a part of you that satisfies your souls' desire. don't shut out inclincations to explore what makes your heart smile; if you listen closely it may be the very thing you need to do.

Adrian Michael

a day without...

strip down to three things that you could not go a day without (exclude the basic necessities of food, water and shelter)—ask yourself, "what makes me happy? what is that one thing that i could spend hours doing and not get bored? if i could make a living doing what i love, what would that be? is my happiness even important? why or why not?

happiness is a way of life and rather than count the hours, live each breath of air and see it as a chancce to see something new, taste something different, feel something magical, and hear something beautiful.

Adrian Michael

mind
---
body

sunday mornings were special. our father would wake up my brother and i to run around the park. some days i didn't feel like running but we had no choice. some things you don't like to do but they turn out to be what is best for you. 3.5 miles. keeping up with our dad was the real challenge.

he would say, "mind over body." you are only tired if you tell yourself you're tired. mind over body. running began to get easier and easier. mind over body. the distance seemed shorter. mind over body. our hearts grew stronger. mind over body. lessons ingrained in our heads.

we think things into existence. thoughts are so powerful: they send positive (and negative) energy throughout our core and limbs and what we feel then pours out. many times i have wanted to stop doing something because i didn't have the mental discipline to see it through but i have reclaimed the mantra, "mind over body," and remind myself that quitting is easy but regret lasts forever.

it works in many things. apply it to the relationship with yourself and with others.

talk through things before you are quick to shut down; consider multiple perspectives before making an uninformed decision; push yourself to reach heights you thought were too high. your soul will be at ease knowing you have done the best you could do. that is what matters most.

be happy.

Adrian Michael

enjoy

if you can't enjoy time with yourself or
enjoy the company you keep with another,
where does happiness exist?

if we did not know sorrow
then we would not know bliss
ying-yang paradigm shift
this life has us on a balance beam
sometimes it's easy to want to jump off
no, get back on and walk life's plank
fall and fall and fall again
get up, get up, get up again
find a state of well-being
happiness
peace of mind

they notice your light
like a one-car collision
only slowing down, or simply passing by
without stopping.
oh, they see you alright
wondering
curious;
some want to dim your light
pull you into darkness
stay on the path
hold up your head
walk tall
the journey is about self-discovery

Adrian Michael

i admire the wind
how it brushes the sky
it creates big and small
gusts
swift enough
powerful enough
to shape and chisel
mountain rock;
be like the wind
flutter about
be you
swim through clouds
dance with trees
know that your presence
is
swift enough
strong enough
to inspire others

NOTES OF A DENVER NATIVE SON

strike a path
through deep-green forest
not with iron fist
or sharp machete
not with intent
to displace or destroy
natural habitat

far too often
we are quick
to uproot, remove, demolish
what it is we think we know
our lack of understanding
is fueled fear
taking iron fists
and sharp machetes
through beautiful things

Adrian Michael

you know that feeling
when you're couped up in the house
with nothing to do
no one to talk to?

you want to do something
but going stir crazy
pacing the house
countless steps

boredom sinks in
too lazy to decide
unsure how to occupy time
the world outside your doorstep—

your soul is on fire
begging
to get out
simply listen
listen close

meet me somewhere
anywhere that you please
i've traveled to your smile
a sunshine state

the railroad tracks
are you sure?
i'll meet you there
the spine of her back

this will be a first
never have i traveled by train

happiness
is a way of life
it's like
learning how
to write

pick up the pencil
make infinite circles
learn the laws of scribbles
on to cursive
eventually

follow an outline
connect those broken lines

find voice
in handwriting

seek inner peace
best you know how
joy comes in the
space between
sunrises
and across
sunsets

reasons to smile:

1. smiling looks good on you
2. puts you in a better mood
3. helps to see the positive in situations that look/feel bad
4. smiling sends contagious energy that spreads like wildfire
5. wakes up the sleeping soul
6. smiling tells part of your story; opens you up to be approachable
7. extends your lifetime: when you share a smile with someone else your name will always be on their lips
8. smiling is physical enthusiasm; anything that comes out of your mouth will contain stars
9. when used for good it is a passport to another's heart
10. like wearing a power tie, a smile is a metaphor

Adrian Michael

city birds
clash
with rush hour traffic
wouldn't they rather
soar and play
where clouds
ice mountaintops?
it's so busy
city living
colorado boulevard
i-25
6th avenue
you can never be alone
not until you hit the countryside
where all you hear
are wing-tipped painters
waiting for
city bird cousins
to arrive

NOTES OF A DENVER NATIVE SON

on a boulder he climbed
against anxious pleas
"those are known to move
   no, no, don't go up there!"
muting the suggestion
he found great footing
and waited for them
to snap a picture
raised his hands to the sky
as if the world had been conquered
and posed
for what would be
his new facebook profile pic

53,000 acres in the round
views profound
flora and fauna
below

"yolo,"
         you only live once
he proclaimed walking away
and they dissappeared from
whence they came

i wonder what version
he will tell
of lookout mountain

how long would it take
to climb each rocky mountain
and bottle that white stuff
in the distant blue?

i'm not quite sure
but i'll go with you
until the last snow melts

that would make me happy
i know it would

a poetic journey to the west
where snow never melts

an honor it must be
for rain to soak your soil first
being this high up
a few miles below the place
where weather is created

being with you is like that
except i'm a mile high
just being next to you
and your soul waters my soul
in any condition

Adrian Michael

trust
that i will
catch you
if you fall
my bones
would fracture first
before harm
comes to you

what makes a thing wild?
roaming around free?
those obsessed with
putting things in cages
are surely the crazies
dealing with whirlwind chaos
rattling inside themselves

what makes a thing wild?
if you can answer that question
your soul is bleeding out

***

you are a wild thing
   too wild to seek approval
you are a free spirit
   too free to need validation
you are a unique soul
   too unique to be compared
you are an exquisite creature
   too exquisite to dim;
live for you
request opinions
but at the end of the day
make decisions
that don't sabotage
being naturally different

Adrian Michael

namaste

the divine in me honors and sees
the divine in you. each soul has
a story that must come up for air: it is
no coincidence that we stumble
upon people and declare each other
kindred spirits, kinfolk, soul mates...
your story, your being, your essence
is playing out in a dimension that
you can't see, only the soul can. it
operates in a world where souls
see souls and only wants to be
around positive energy. so when you
encounter someone and it feels as
though you have known them all
of your life, but just met, you
actually have known them—it's just
that your souls have interacted
long before you knew them
in this place.

honor each other in love & light, the world
is better off for it. negative energy can
only withstand so much and sooner or
later it will have to convert to positive
energy or retreat.

let your soul thrive and exist in freedom.

namaste.

i am happy.
truly, happy.
happiness
is not
deficient

be kind
always.
isn't that
the
golden rule?
it's said
in many ways
and in numerous
languages and tongues

be golden
be kind
if you forget
all the rest
do not forget
this:
live
love
&
be happy

everything else
will fall
into place

denver
you have
such mood
swings
four seasons
in a day
snow-capped
mountains
to the west
a mile high
above the rest.
what i love most
about my city
is
not the pavillions
pete's kitchen or diner
nor the skyline
civic center or marade
festivals, block parties or
jazz in the park—
it's that
you often give
tourists
such
altitude
sickness
making native lungs
prepared
for any
elevation.
our 300 days of sunshine
melts snow
and hearts
you'll find love here
i fell in love here

NOTES OF A DENVER NATIVE SON

vera collier. elizabeth gautier. joyce lynn. larry p. gautier. opalonga pugh. robert williams. j.douglass vaughn-harris. maya angelou.

Ase'

Share your notes with me #NOADNS

I would love to get any feedback and connect.

email: adrianmichaelgreen@gmail.com
web: adrianmichaelgreen.com

magic
happens when YOU
DO what
you
are going to do.

SAY

adrian michael

@adrianmichaelgreen
@adrianmichaelgr

ABOUT DENVER'S NATIVE SON

A native of Northeast Denver, Adrian Michael Green is committed to giving back to the community. Considering himself a creative enthusiast, Adrian works in all things multimedia and connects his passion of expression to help others tell their story while continuing to share his own. Editor of No Witty, a literary and visual arts magazine, he has steadfast ambition to feature and publish talented artists worldwide.

Adrian is a writer, photographer, public speaker, businessman, educator and author; using his pen name, Adrian Michael, he has self-published three other books.

Made in the USA
Monee, IL
16 July 2020